Y0-CBZ-264

UNSUNG HEROES OF THE CIVIL RIGHTS MOVEMENT AND THEREAFTER

Profiles of Lessons Learned

Edited by
Dorothy M. Singleton

University Press of America,® Inc.
Lanham • Boulder • New York • Toronto • Plymouth, UK

Copyright © 2014 by University Press of America,® Inc.
4501 Forbes Boulevard, Suite 200, Lanham, Maryland 20706
UPA Aquisitions Department (301) 459-3366

10 Thornbury Road, Plymouth PL6 7PP, United Kingdom

Library of Congress Control Number: 2013957045
ISBN: 978-0-7618-6318-2 (cloth : alk. paper)—ISBN: 978-0-7618-6319-9 (electronic)

∞™ The paper used in this publication meets the minimum requirements of American National Standard for Information Sciences Permanence of Paper for Printed Library Materials, ANSI/NISO Z39.48-1992.

CONTENTS

FOREWORD

Jonathan N. Livingston, Ph.D.

Although America is 40 years removed from the turmoil of the 1960's, the people, policies and their vision for a better America continue to impact and shape our world today. From Dr. Martin Luther King, Jr.'s letters from the Birmingham jail to the speeches and writings from Baynard Rustin, Roy Wilkings and Stokely Carmichael, we have heard their rallying call for change. Although their speeches and writings have shed light on the political and ideological thinking of the times, the work of many southern activist and organizers has not been thoroughly examined.

Dr. Singleton's book will shed light on the contributions of these young people who risked their lives to gain access to the ideals that America had promised. Through nonviolent protest, community education and advocacy, they were successful in securing social and political justice for those marginalized by Jim Crowism and other forms of racial injustices.

Dr. Singleton's book showcases the contributions and struggles of those forgotten by popular press, but yet, in the 1960's swept by the zeitgeist of the times, they were compelled to define their existence in the struggle to be simply recognized as human beings. This book is a must read for young student activists/scholars, as well as those who wish to better understand the complexities of the Civil Rights Movement and the lives of those who experienced it.

Jonathan N. Livingston, Ph.D.
Department of Psychology
North Carolina Central University

INTRODUCTION

The Civil Rights Movement brought forth many heroes who set an example for America and the world. Reverend Dr. Martin Luther King, Jr., Rosa Parks, the Reverend Jesse Jackson, and Andrew Young are household names. While all who participated in the movement earned a rightful place in society, many did not get the recognition they deserved, and others were virtually unknown. This book is about several of those unsung heroes: the Saint Augustine Four, Rachel Robinson, and Emmett Till.

This book will afford people the opportunity to learn more about these important individuals who offered much to America but were overlooked or forgotten, despite their memorable deeds. The book will cover The Saint Augustine Four (Audrey Nell Edwards, JoeAnn Anderson Olmer, Willie Carl Singleton, and Samuel White), a group of individuals who participated in a "sit-in" at a Woolworth's store; Emmett Till, a 14-year old African American male murdered in Money, Mississippi, an event considered one of the principal factors leading to the Civil Rights Movement; Rachel Robinson, wife of the late Jackie Robinson, who has continued his legacy through the Jackie Robinson Foundation; Irene Morgan Kirkaldy, who refused to give up her seat on a city bus in Gloucester County, Virginia (1944); and Stokely Carmichael, a Trinidadian American who became the leader of the Student Nonviolent Coordinating Committee (SNCC).

This book can be related to or compared with other works in the field-such as *Picking Cotton: Our Memoir of Injustice and Redemption* by Jennifer-Thompson-Cannino and Howard Zinn's book, *The People Speak: American Voices, Some Famous, Some Little Known*.

I

IRENE MORGAN KIRKALDY

Freedom, Bravery and Justice

By Dorothy Hines, Ph.D. Candidate,
Michigan State University

Irene Morgan Kirkaldy is known as the original *Freedom Rider* who rebelled against Jim Crow during a Greyhound bus trip in 1944. She altered the Virginia state transportation law on what appeared to be a normal day. During Irene's travel from Virginia to Baltimore, Maryland, she sat in the Colored section of the bus as indicated by transportation regulations. As the Greyhound traveled to Baltimore to pick up passengers, Irene Morgan Kirkaldy was asked to sit in the back of the bus to allow White passengers access to her seat. The decision *not* to sit in the back of the bus, although, the same choice that Rosa Parks made years later, was for a much different reason. Irene Morgan Kirklady refused to give up her seat because bus laws in Virginia and Maryland failed to apply across state lines. This incident led to efforts by the National Association for the Advancement of Colored People (NAACP) and Irene to change interstate transportation policies that ultimately went to the Supreme Court in 1946 and the enforcement of Jim Crow.

Born in Gloucester County, Virginia, Irene Morgan Kirklady was one of nine children raised by her mother and father in a working class Black neighborhood. As a painter, her father lived in the era of the Great Depression while her mother cared for Irene's younger siblings. Raised in the household of a Seventh - day Adventist, Irene lived in segregated Maryland where she dropped out of high school to assist with the costs of living for her family. Irene's father financially struggled to raise her family resulting in her decision to work jobs as a maid and various other household duties for pay. As a child, Irene's religious surroundings coupled with her parent's socialization of her as a Black female in a racially and socially segregated state, propelled her to be active in issues impacting the African American communities. Her upbringing largely exposed her to the realities of racial and socioeconomic inequalities that Blacks experienced in the North and South while conditioning her to have positive self-efficacy and confidence in her role in changing society for the betterment of her community. Irene was an active civil rights leader and was involved in a 1946 case of Irene Morgan v. State of Virginia. A United States Supreme Court ruling declared that forced segregation of an interstate bus was illegal. The Supreme Court ruling played a critical role in her ability to resist giving up her seat and challenge state law based on her civil rights.

Before suffering a miscarriage in July 1944, twenty-seven-year-old Irene went to visit her mother in Gloucester County. After leaving Maryland and traveling to Baltimore, Irene sat in the Colored section of the bus. However, White-only sections of the Greyhound were limited to the number of Whites requesting seats were the section was extended for Whites on the bus. As Whites sat on the bus, Irene was required to move to another seat but refused. Irene's refusal resulted in the bus driver's summons of the police and her arrest. Consequently, not giving up her seat was based on the absence of policy to dictate racial segregation on state buses. Irene's decision to stay seated was a question of the constitutionality of an African American sitting in designated White passenger seats.

Irene's refusal to give her seat to a White passenger caused alarm on the bus with Blacks and Whites. The bus driver traveled to the next stop where sheriffs were waiting to apprehend Irene Morgan. A Black woman on the bus suggested to Irene to relocate to avoid confrontation. However, she decided to keep her seat as state law did not determine racial segregation on interstate transportation services. Commotion resulted on the bus and at the next stop the police were waiting. Irene was dragged off the Greyhound and apprehended by police. During the arrest, Irene's confrontation with the police led to her arrest. In resisting, Irene injured a police officer (Kirk, 2009). Fined a $100 charge for assaulting police, Irene contacted the NAACP after her arrest.

In Irene's arraignment, the judge contended that she pay the $100 assault fine and determined that Irene was guilty of violating Virginia state law. There was a warrant out for Irene's arrest as she decided whether to contest the incident. At district court, Irene paid the fine but contested her arrest for violation of state law. Her concerns were expressed to the NAACP in addition to other organizations that supported the rights of Black citizens. The NAACP included Thurgood Marshall who was a trained attorney and who was knowledgeable of the legal system. The NAACP and Congress of Racial Equality (CORE) worked to address avenues for arguing Irene's case.

The incident raised questions about the utility of transportation laws extending to surrounding states. The bus driver's request to Irene (i.e. "You'll have to get up and give your seat to these people") (Arsenault, 2005) suggested that she was undermining Jim Crow policies and failing to allow White passengers certain rights and privileges in interstate busing. Under Jim Crow, Blacks were provided limited rights in public spaces. During district court proceedings, Irene explained why she resisted arrest. Irene's recount of the arrest portrayed the police as aggressors who kicked her and used more force than necessary. She contended:

> He touched me. That's when I kicked him in a very bad place. He hobbled off, and another one came on. He was trying to put his hands on me to get me off. I was going to bite him, but he was dirty, so I clawed him instead. I ripped his shirt. We were both pulling at each other. He said he'd use his nightstick. I said, "We'll whip each other" (Arsenault, 2005).

In the end, it took both officers to subdue her, and when she complained that they were hurting her arms, the deputy shouted, "Wait till I get you to jail, I'll beat your head with a stick" (Arsenault, 2005).

Blacks were viewed in stereotypical ways (Arsenault, 2005). Released on a $500 bond, Irene explained the event to the NAACP. She stated, "I was just minding my own business. I'd paid my money. I was just sitting where I was supposed to sit. And I wasn't going to take it" (Arsenault, 2005). Irene's discussion with the NAACP, coupled with experiences that Blacks conveyed under Jim Crow, created a timely opportunity for the NAACP to challenge her arrest. The NAACP was vying for a chance to undermine race-based policies that prohibited Blacks from full citizenship. This injustice was not exclusive to the transportation industry but included social equity in employment, housing, and racial inclusiveness. Thurgood Marshall believed that the removal of Irene from her seat was unconstitutional, since there were limited laws that protected the state of Virginia in her arrest. Specifically, interstate transportation included Greyhound buses and other means of travel from one state to another. Since there were no laws that dictated Jim Crow across state lines, it would be difficult for Virginia to justify Irene's arrest.

As Irene further discussed the incident with the NAACP and CORE, the necessity for social movement to counter Jim Crow practices became more evident. Lead by Thurgood Marshall, the NAACP contended that current segregation laws failed to account for interstate transportation. With the absence of policies addressing busing across state lines, Irene was not breaking the law. Therefore it was not unconstitutional to resist moving to another section of the bus, given in the District of Columbia at this particular time period, the city did not have a policy regarding segregated bus transportation. This gap was the avenue of appeal the NAACP used to appeal the court's conviction of Irene for resisting Jim Crow mandates. In Irene's appeal to the Supreme Court, the NAACP asserted that racially segregated spaces are not transferable to other states that fail to have

Jim Crow policies and practices. The appeal went to the Supreme Court in *Irene Morgan v. Commonwealth of Virginia* in 1946.

Appealing to the Supreme Court was a difficult task for Irene as she was basing her claims on the absence of law to address interstate busing. This legal oversight provided an outlet for her to challenge her arrest. Petitions to the Supreme Court were accepted as Marshall moved Irene's case further through the judicial system. The social movement spurred by Irene's case provided utility for Blacks to ride on integrated state transportation systems. Winning this case would foster Thurgood Marshall's legal efforts to create new social opportunities for Black communities. The mission of the NAACP and CORE is to ensure the political, educational, social, and economic equality of rights of all individuals and to eliminate race-based discrimination. A core element of this case was to ensure social justice in places where it was not adequately served to Blacks. This inequality was evident in various forms of society and, by challenging state transportation systems; it would create a hedge in Jim Crow.

Proponents of Irene and Marshall crafted a case that enforced previous Supreme Court rulings while focusing on holes in current law. This process consisted of visiting cases in which the court ruled in favor of Blacks. These cases included racial segregation and transportation. In 1946, the court case *Morgan v. Commonwealth of Virginia* challenged the absence of segregated transportation across state borders. Using previous court cases as a fundamental component of the *Morgan* case, various arguments were used to contend Irene's innocence. These cases, coupled with social support from Black communities, provided additional support for the plaintiffs and swayed the judges' opinions. The ruling of *Morgan* reinforced the role of state law that prohibited Jim Crow in states that allowed its existence.

The 1896 Supreme Court case *Plessey v. Ferguson* was a critical argument of the NAACP's case. *Plessey* challenged the use of racially segregated public spaces as constitutional in states where it was not enforced. *Plessey v. Ferguson* provided the "infamous doctrine of separate but equal, which gave constitutional legitimacy to Jim Crow segregation laws" (Golub, 2005). While *Plessey* focused on public space, it was not inclusive of interstate transportation. The *Morgan* case suggested "no state law can reach beyond its own border nor bar transportation of passengers across its boundaries, diverse seating requirements for the races in interstate journeys result" (Pilgrim, 2007). This gap in the Supreme Court's ruling left space for ambiguity in how busing segregation would apply across state lines. This favored Irene as federal law did not addressed this issue. In general, Irene would not be in violation of interstate policies that did not exist.

Another case used to support Irene's argument was *Mitchell v. Arkansas* 1941. This court case challenged the role of racial segregation in intrastate busing services ruling in the favor of a Black male passenger (Golub, 2005). The court rulings supported Irene who contended that federal and state law did not determine segregation across state lines. This ruling provided Marshall a method for using transportation rulings and racial issues to press for an overturn of Irene's previous case. The issue of interstate transportation and law had not been decided on or visited by the Supreme Court. Irene's case, presumed by the NAACP, had a chance to alter how the courts and states were required to treat Black passengers in opposition to Jim Crow. Ruling in favor of Irene was presumed to provide equal access to Blacks in transportation and then to other social avenues. Generally, there were mixed messages about the utility of the NAACP and Irene contesting her arrest if state and district laws remained racially segregated and based on inequitable standards. There was uncertainty regarding the influence of the case. Whether it would be immediate or in the future could not yet be determined. President Truman and other federal and state officials paid minimal attention to the ruling as it appeared to be a small victory in changing U.S. racial relations.

The *Morgan* decision was handed down by the Supreme Court on June 3, 1946. The anticipation of the case was a state concern and a national issue. As the nation became focused on the case, the ruling became more critical to race relations and segregated policies in the North. The Supreme Court ruled 7-1 that the state of Virginia illegally enforced racial segregation across its borders. This was a vital victory for the NAACP, Irene Morgan Kirklady, and Blacks across the United States. As the *Morgan case* ruling spread cross the North and South, Blacks celebrated a critical movement toward racial inclusion. The court opinion "decreed that segregation in interstate travel was "an undue burden on interstate commerce" (Houser, 2006). This opinion supported Irene's movement for social equity. The 1947 freedom song *You Don't Have to Ride Jim Crow* surfaced in celebration of the *Morgan case.* The song was sung:

> "You don't have to ride jim crow,
> You don't have to ride jim crow,
> Get on the bus, set any place,

'Cause Irene Morgan won her case,
You don't have to ride jim crow."

The victory achieved with *Morgan* set the stage for the NAACP to focus on other legal issues in the Black communities. The overall perception was that Jim Crow was revealed to the nation and that this opened new opportunities for society to focus on other civil rights issues. It was Irene's victory and Marshall's victory that was celebrated. However, the movement in the courts was lengthy and largely remained unsettled after the case. Celebration in not riding Jim Crow was short-lived as de facto segregation continued decades later.

The results of Irene's case favored her petition that treatment was unconstitutional. Publication of the *Morgan case* varied in the North and the South. In the South, "editors and reporters downplayed the significance of the Court's ruling" (Arsenault, 2005), while in other areas, there was limited explanation of positive conclusions from the case. After the ruling, favoritism for *Morgan* began to diminish. Political backlash mounted from policymakers and state officials who had to implement *Morgan*. The *Morgan case* resulted in further contention between races as officials had to develop new procedures for busing across state lines. Additional animosity was created for White passengers who often favored Jim Crow and its privileges at the expense of equity and social justice. The transportation industry valued equality but not equity as evident in the *Plessey v. Ferguson* ruling. Separate but equal could not be legitimized in states where Jim Crow expectations were not valid. Such legal inconsistency created a challenging position for Blacks as they followed one standard for busing services in one state and then another as they crossed state lines. The ruling impacted how and if Morgan would be a daily expectation.

There were several factors that impacted the implementation of *Morgan*. The *Morgan* case was accorded during the end of World War II and prior to *Brown v. Board of Education* 1954. Race relations were at an all-time high after WWII and entering into *Brown* which was presumed to integrate public schools. Resistance by Whites grew during the 20th century to block social equality for Black. The impact of this resistance influenced the viability of *Morgan* as a predominant concern to the nation. For some states, the case was not influential. Uncertainty in the case's ruling simply led to further ambiguity in the strength of the decision in being enforced on a national scale.

A primary issue that arouse after the case was how to implement policy when people resisted at various levels. In North Carolina, Stanley Winborne, the utilities commissioner, acknowledged it would be a "regrettable decision to require bus companies to halt the practice of Jim Crowing on interstate runs" (Arsenault, 2005). Comparable statements were echoed by other states in resisting *Morgan*. In Louisiana, Clayton Coleman, Public Service Commissioner, contended segregation among "intrastate passengers will continue to be enforced and that even among interstate passengers no racial mixing would be allowed until the Interstate Commerce Commission (ICC) validated the *Morgan* ruling" (Arsenault, 2005). How states would decide on whether to implement *Morgan*, given additional pressures from Whites and the political strength of their presence in the political system, resulted in *Morgan* not being fully realized.

Prior to Rosa Parks' refusal to move from her seat, decades earlier, Irene Morgan Kirklady started a social movement in Virginia that traveled to the Supreme Court. Although the efforts of Irene, Thurgood Marshall, and the NAACP did not fully come into fruition, her legacy continues. In 1991, Bill Clinton stated that Irene Morgan Kirklady was the original Rosa Parks who started a movement that has not fully been realized on a national scale. Irene was ambitiously motivated to stand for her beliefs of social justice and equity on transportation services long before other Black women. Prior to Irene's death, she was recognized by local, state, and national officials for her courageous stance against Jim Crow and her willingness to fight for individual and collective justice at any costs. Her accomplishment not only provided more than access to equal transportation services for Blacks, but it also encouraged others, including Rosa Parks, to stand against Jim Crow policies and practices.

On August 10, 2007, Irene's death reignited her passionate movement for social equality in interstate transportation and social justice. Her efforts to fight segregated busing policies across state lines set the stage for additional movements by African Americans to establish equity in the legal system and on a national scale. Her induction in the Maryland Women's Hall of Fame and receipt of the President Citizens Medal, in 2001, the second highest award in the U.S., demonstrate that her commitment to fighting against injustices was not overlooked. Irene Morgan Kirkaldy died at the age of 90.

FOR FURTHER DISCUSSION

Irene was involved in many events related to civil rights and social justice issues. The following are questions which individuals can engage in discussions about this inspiring lady.

1. How can social movements be framed after social justice produce inequitable outcomes?
2. What is the legacy of Irene Morgan Kirkaldy for Whites today? How is equity a collective rather than an individual goal?
3. Describe how racial tensions shape efforts to sustain social justice. What role can state and federal policy play in sustaining social change?
4. How were Black and White people affected by Jim Crow laws during the time of segregation?

REFERENCES

Golub, M. (2005). Plessey as "Passing": Judicial Responses to Ambiguously Raced Bodies in Plessey v. Ferguson. Law & Society Review39. 3 (Sep 2005): 563-600.

Houser, G. (2006). Freedom Riders: 1961 and the struggle for racial justice fellowship. 72. 9-12. 42-43.

Kirk, J. (2009). The Long Road to Equality. History Today59. 2. 52-58.

Lackey, P. (2001). The Virginian-Pilot Newspaper: Norfolk, VA.

Pilgrim, D. (2007). Irene Morgan v. Commonwealth of Virginia. Jim Crow Museum of Racist Memorabilia. Ferris State University: Retrieved from http://www.ferris.edu/jimcrow/question/dec07/.

2

EMMETT LOUIS TILL

Young, Innocent, and Vulnerable

By Dorothy M. Singleton, Ph.D.,
North Carolina Central University

INTRODUCTION

During the 1950s and 1960s, there were turbulent times for African Americans, especially in the south where Jim Crow laws were prevalent; a time of racial hatred and hardships. Those of us who grew up as children in the 1950-1960s eras; racism was at its peak. African Americans and Whites were divided in a nation which all people should have equal rights. We learned much over the years about separation of races and cultures in America. As I reflect on what took place during the twentieth century and the radical change African Americans encountered, it was devastating to say the least. African Americans were searching for the freedom they knew nothing about when slavery finally ended and doubts of moving forward were unthinkable at the time. It was psychological trauma, initially, to be free and having to be a problem-solver for their own lives. The experience of not being told what to do and how to do it caused mass confusion in not having an overseer or slave owner to tell them what to do. There was a lack of leadership *from* African Americans *for* African Americans. Maloney (2001) stated that "despite these dramatic developments, many economic and demographic characteristics of African Americans at the end of the nineteenth century were not that different from what they had been in the mid-1800s." To be human for an African American was to be dehumanized by Whites. This treatment dated back to the time of slavery. African Americans were treated like animals and were ridiculed, beaten and killed. In many instances, the tormentor got away with these crimes with little less than a slap on the wrist. They were constantly being dehumanized and stigmatized by Whites. African Americans were viewed by Whites as a disease. They were kept suppressed in the south by behaviors that were unbecoming to the human race as a whole. Later on, throughout the 19th and 20th century, African Americans struggled to gain their freedom. Freedom was always about having responsibility. African Americans knew that with great freedom, comes great power. There was always a bright light at the end of the tunnel for them. During the 1890s, African Americans left the south, in great numbers, to move north or to the Midwest. They hoped that by leaving the south there would be more opportunities for a new start for their families. Indifferences and turmoil came to a crescendo and during the early 1950s African Americans felt neglected, deprived, and had no sense of belonging in a society they felt had failed them.

THE MOVE TO ILLINOIS: THE CARTHAN FAMILY

Mamie Carthan was a young African American female born during the time when social injustice was an issue and a part of the society in which she lived in; living in an environment that epitomized White people, in America, as being privileged. Mamie's family moved from a little town near Webb, Mississippi when she was a very young girl. The south was not a good fit for them. Her mother knew that if she wanted what was best for her daughter, Mississippi was not the place to raise a child; especially an African American child.

Mamie was the only child born to John and Alma Carthan on November 23, 1921. After Mamie's parents were married for several years, they divorced when she was 13 years old (Till-Mobley & Benson, 2003). Mamie was raised in a very sheltered environment. Once the family moved to Argo, Illinois, many of her immediate family moved from Mississippi as well. Mamie was an intelligent young girl who was determined to be a productive citizen. She was obedient and a very dutiful member of the church.

As years passed, Mamie graduated from a predominately white school, Argo Community High School. After graduation, she married Louis Till. They were a loving couple who shared a common bond of love and friendship. Louis was the love of her life. Two years later a baby was born to this union. A baby boy named Emmett Louis Till. He was born on July 25, 1941. Mamie and Louis were ecstatic to have given birth to a baby boy. "It was a difficult birth" as Mamie later said to her many friends and family as she talked about her precious child; however, Mamie called Emmett her "miracle baby" (Till-Mobley & Benson, 2003). Mamie's baby had several medical problems from the beginning of birth due to being a breech baby. Mamie's husband was away often; traveling as an amateur boxer and working at the local corn product factory. Later on in their marriage, Louis was called to active duty in the arm forces. He was deployed to Italy as an Army Private. Unfortunately, Louis was killed when he was stationed in Italy. Mamie's life continued on. She was determined to provide the very best for her little boy. She was a dedicated mother with a lot of pride. Two years after her husband's death, Mamie married Gene "Pink" Bradley, but only for a short period of time.

When Emmett was 5 years of age he contracted polio, but soon that illness was no longer an existing problem. Later on in life, he was diagnosed as being a stutterer. Stuttering would remain a part of Emmett's life. Mamie would tell him to "take in a breath, whistle, and then go ahead and speak." Of course, when Emmett spoke, a whistling sound was projected from his words" (Till-Mobley & Benson, 2003). However, Emmett accepted any challenge that confronted him. The stuttering didn't bother Emmett…he was one who loved to talk and would speak with confidence with his family and friends. Emmett was an amazing boy with great potential to be whatever he wanted to be during this era. Mamie, at times, would reference Emmett as "Bo;" fondly…it was his nickname.

Mamie, Mrs. Alma Carthan, and Emmett were very close. Mrs. Carthan, Emmett's maternal grandmother was very strict; however, Mamie liked the way her mother raised her and wanted Emmett to be raised the same way…strict, but loving and patient. Mamie wanted what was best for him. She wanted him to be respectful, kind, patient and considerate to others. Emmett felt that "there was a solution to every problem and through this awareness of solving problems; he developed a positive attitude towards people. No one was a stranger to him" (Till-Mobley & Benson, 2003).

Mamie and her mother were surrounded by family members and others who moved from Mississippi to Illinois. Mamie felt that her mother's house was a stopping point for many Mississippians. Mamie was a woman of confidence, too. Mamie's relatives were very likable people (Till-Mobley & Benson, 2003).

Emmett was developing into a more capable child. "Mamie lavished Emmett with clothes and just about anything she wanted for him" (Till-Mobley & Benson, 2003). She was willing to do as much as possible to make Emmett happy. Emmett was beginning to develop a personality of his own. He was a very engaging child; always looking for something to do; "It had become obvious to Mamie and her mother that there was no problem Emmett wouldn't try to solve, no difficulty he wouldn't try to overcome. "Emmett was very industrious" (Till-Mobley & Benson, 2003). He was in junior high and was in his teens. School was immensely exciting for Emmett. Mamie showered his son with many material things in life. She wanted the best for him. In many instances, Mamie treated Emmett more like a younger brother. Mamie bought a new car and Emmett was given the opportunity to a "trial drive" of it. She wanted to please Emmett and he wanted to please his mother.

He was friendly and was, in many cases, the center of attention when he was surrounded by his friends and family. Emmett was a jokester and a natural leader (Till-Mobley & Benson, 2003). There was an aura that people liked about him. He was handsome and also a stylish dresser. Emmett was an eighth grader and was 14 years of age. He was restless at times, spending most of his time in Argo and Chicago, Illinois. He was ready to visit other family members in Money, Mississippi. His cousins, in Argo, were talking about visiting family in Mississippi. Emmett was eager to hear about the planned trip. He was excited. However, the thought of sharing this trip with his mother was overbearing. He was a young man ready to experience what life offered on his own. Emmett had only been away from his mother for a short period of time when she was working in Detroit, Michigan for the Social Security Administration. Emmett lived with his grandmother and Mamie would travel from Detroit to Chicago to visit with him during the weekends.

MAMIE'S CONCERNS ABOUT EMMETT'S TRAVEL TO MISSISSIPPI

Mamie felt it was time for a family trip. She wanted to travel to Detroit and then to Omaha, Nebraska (Till-Mobley & Benson, 2003). Emmett saw differently. He wanted to go to Mississippi with his cousins and Uncle Mose. He was eagerly looking forward to this trip. Emmett was 14 years of age now and wanted to explore another direction for a summer getaway. He was looking forward to a new environment; different people in a different setting. Mamie was adamant about Emmett's travel to the Mississippi where there was racial hatred and Emmett being naïve to White people of the south. Mamie felt uneasy about the idea of Emmett wanting to go to Mississippi:

The answer was no. Absolutely not. I was against it, my mother was against it. No matter how much people were talking Mississippi this and Mississippi that, we did not want Emmett to go unless he could go with one of us, as he had done a couple of times before when he was much younger (Till-Mobley & Benson, 2003).

Emmett had his mind set on going to Mississippi regardless of what his mother said to him. He was not giving in to her reasons for him not going with his cousins and Uncle Mose. Mamie had always wanted the best for Emmett but was not willing to separate from him even if it was a trip to visit family; she felt a need to protect him. He was her only child; he was everything to her.

However, Mamie finally approved of letting Emmett travel to Mississippi with much hesitation. She asked Uncle Mose to watch Emmett on a regular basis and for him to not get too much away from him. Mamie told Emmett how to respond to white people…in other words …know how to act properly:

> Then, he went on to remind me of things I had taught him, things I had told him as a child, things he assured me he always did. If he was talking to an adult out in Argo, there was a proper way to do it. As he walked around out there, he had to speak politely to everyone he saw. And he was taught to answer anyone speaking to him by saying, "Yes, Mrs. So-and-So," or "No, Mrs. So-and-So." Never just "yes" or "no" (Till-Mobley & Benson, 2003).

Mamie endured that mother's intuition which caused concerns she had about this trip. She knew something was not right. Emmett was warned about the ways of the south

(Till-Mobley & Benson, 2003). She knew Emmett was not ready for this trip…thinking about the racial attitudes of White people in the south. Emmett was naïve of the culture of the south. Mamie was paralyzed by the thought of allowing her son to take this trip. Emmett knew very little about the deep-south and how totally different it was from Chicago. African Americans in the south lived in separate communities…far away from White people. Emmett took pictures of his school mates and other items of interest to share with his family and family friends. Emmett was not fearful much of anything; he had confidence in doing just about what he wanted to achieve in life. He was a boy from Chicago who was known by many and liked by all throughout his community. He felt safe in Chicago and any other locations he visited. Emmett came from a happy, supportive, and loving family and a positive community environment. However, Mississippi was to be proven totally different from his safe environment. The state of Mississippi was going through some turbulent times. Racism ran rampage throughout the south. Jim Crowism ideologies were embedded in the south. There was no way of getting around it. The people were divided along racial lines.

EMMETT'S TRIP TO MONEY, MISSISSIPPI

Emmett was excited about his visit to Money, Mississippi. As a fourteen year old boy, away from his mother, was a new found excitement for Emmett. He was traveling with his cousins Wheeler Parker, Curtis Jones, and his Uncle Mose to a city which he hadn't visited since he was a toddler. It was on Saturday, August 20, 1955, they left, by train, on their journey. They arrived in Money, Mississippi on August 21st. Emmett's cousins were accustomed to doing fieldwork. Emmett agreed to work in the cotton field with them. However, Emmett had a different orientation of doing work…not picking cotton. At a later time during his visit with his cousins, he chose to do chores inside the house. Nevertheless, the following event took place:

> On Monday morning August 22nd, Emmett and his cousins began picking cotton for his great-uncle, Mose Wright, a sharecropper whose farm was near Money, Mississippi. On Wednesday, August 24th, Emmett (14), along with Simeon (12), Maurice (16), Wheeler Parker (16), Roosevelt Crawford (15) and Ruthie Mae Crawford (18), went into the town of Money, Mississippi after a day of picking cotton (Beauchamp, 2005).

On Wednesday, August 24th, the cousins had completed their chores for the day. They decided to drive into Money, Mississippi to spend some money on some tasty goodies at the local grocery and market store. As usual, there were other African American young folks gathered for conversation. Doing the time of Jim Crowism, African Americans were only allowed to enter a White-owned store one at a time. A group was never accepted to enter. They followed the chain of command. After the others had purchased their goods, Emmett entered the store. Afterwards, chaos followed. Emmett whistled at the White woman, Carolyn Bryant, wife of the owner of the store. It is hard to believe Emmett would perform such an act due to his mother telling him *right* and *wrong* things to do when visiting relatives in the deep-south; his behavior had to be impeccable. They exited the premise quickly. Emmett did not want his cousins to tell Uncle Mose what took place at the grocery and market place. They swore to secrecy. What followed this incident was unbelievable.

DEMISE OF EMMETT LOUIS TILL

"On August 27 at 9:30pm Mamie Till got a phone call. Several men had come to Uncle Mose's house and had taken Emmett away for questioning about the "whistle" incident that took place earlier that evening at Bryant's Grocery and Market Store. Mamie was terrified. It was, to her, every mother's nightmare to hear something like that about your child" (Till-Mobley & Benson, 2003). To Mamie, it wasn't time to sleep. Her son was heavily on her mind. She was asking many questions. "Maybe this was a mix-up…there must be some confusion…it can't be my son…my only child…my baby" (Till-Mobley & Benson, 2003). The very next morning, Mamie had to make contact with Uncle Mose to get more details about what had taken place in regards to Emmett and why.

One can't even imagine how Mamie felt during this critical time in her life; her only child she was very close to…there was a strong bond between the two of them. Argo and Chicago, Illinois were familiar places for Emmett and his mother. Mamie was very protective of Emmett and loved the times she spent with him. Every moment with him was special to her as it would be for any mother whose child enjoyed life and people.

Three days later, on August 31st, Emmett's body was found floating in the Tallahatchie River. His body was mutilated. Mamie was notified that her son had been found. She was hoping that he was still alive. As we well know, the news was devastating. The family was in a state of shock, disbelief. Emmett's body was shipped to Chicago for burial. Thousands of people were there for the viewing of Emmett's body. The casket was opened for public viewing. Many dignitaries came to show respect for Emmett and his family.

> Some of the dignitaries were Representative Charles Diggs of Detroit, Field Secretary for Mississippi Branch of the NAACP, Medgar Evers, and Dr. T.R.M. Howard who was a civil rights legend in Mississippi and one of the wealthiest African Americans in the state, just to name a few (Till-Mobley & Benson, 2003).

Emmett's burial took place at the Burr Oak Cemetery on September 6, 1955. The murder of Emmett Louis Till brought about world-wide attention. Criminal acts were happening to African Americans in the United States, and especially in the deep-south.

The accusers, Roy Bryant and J.W. Milan, went to trial on September 19th in Sumner, Mississippi. Mamie was there with other close relatives. This trial was a frenzy. Media and journalists were there from all over the world. And on September 23, an all-White male jury found both accusers innocent (Beauchamp, 2005). This was the start of the Civil Rights Movement, knowing that justice was not served in the murder of Emmett Till. Mamie would keep her son's murder alive. She was going to seek justice through the National Association for the Advancement of Colored People (NAACP) and other civil rights groups. Mamie remained active to keep what happened to her son in the forefront of the news.

Before the murder of Emmett Till, landmark civil rights cases before the U.S. Supreme Court were concerned about segregated schools across the nation. It was declared that segregated schools were in violation of one's 14th amendment and deemed as unconstitutional. This ruling took place on May 17, 1954 "simply guaranteeing the right of equality in the American society." Three months later, Rosa Parks made headline news in Montgomery, Alabama. She refused to give up her seat, on a city bus, to a White man. Many other incidences took place all over the United States. African Americans were standing up for their rights…civil rights. Emmett Louis Till's murder sparked many Civil rights events and issues across the nation. It was a start of an intense movement to bring about social change (Beauchamp, 2005). Some of the other landmark cases included ones which covered interstate travel; bus boycotts; special events; and the Civil Rights Act of 1964.

> On November 7, 1955, the U.S. Supreme Court rules segregation in public recreational facilities unconstitutional; on November 25, 1955, The Interstate Commerce Commission bans segregation in interstate travel; on December 5, 1955, the Montgomery Bus Boycott begins and Dr. Martin Luther King, Jr. gives his first civil rights speech in Montgomery, Alabama; on February 3, 1956, Dr. Martin Luther King, Jr. becomes president of the Montgomery Improvement Association (MIA); The Civil Rights Act of 1957 was developed and inspired by the Emmett Till murder; on August 28, 1963, Dr. Martin Luther King, Jr. gives his "I Have a Dream" speech at the March on Washington; and on July 2, 1964, President

Lyndon B. Johnson signs the Civil Rights Act of 1964 banning discrimination in places of public accommodation, barring unequal voter registration requirements, eliminating segregation in federally assisted programs, and setting up the Equal Employment Opportunity Commission (EEOC) (Beauchamp, 2005).

Was there justice in the case? According to the Declaration of Independence of the Constitution of the United States, all men are created equal. They are endowed by their Creator with certain unalienable rights and among these are Life, Liberty and the pursuit of Happiness. Many horrific injustices happened in the life of Emmett Louis Till. The following questions can help stimulate further discussions.

QUESTIONS

1. Emmett Louis Till was a victim of the times during the 1950's era. Why did this have to happen to him in another state which was foreign to him? Was he simply naïve?
2. What can we say about social justice during this time period?
3. If Emmett Louis Till had lived today (2013), would he had been more accepting in this "so-called" liberated society?
4. Did Emmett Till deserve to die from brutal hands of any human being?
5. For many years, Emmett's murder was considered a "cold case." However, many people of Money, Mississippi knew who the killers were at that time. Is it right

to say that Emmett got out of place (meaning that he flirted with a white woman)? Why or why not?

REFERENCES

Beauchamp, K. A. (2005). "The Untold Story of Emmett Louis Till." A Documentary on DVD Video by The Freedom Come Productions, LLC: THINKFilm.

Maloney, T.N. (2001): "Migration and Economic Opportunity in the 1910s: New evidence on African-American occupational mobility in the north;" Journal Explorations in Economic History, 38, 147-165. Elsevier.com.

Till-Mobley, M. & Benson, C. (2003). Death of Innocence: The story of the hate crime that changed America. The Random House Publishing Group: New York: NY.

Till-Mobley, M. (spring, 2003), 1920-2002 "Mamie Mobley Till" The Journal of Blacks in Higher Education, No. 39 p. 89 Retrieved from http://www.jstor.org/stable/3134389.

3

THE SAINT AUGUSTINE FOUR

Living Life on the Edge

By Nancy Reese-Durham, Ph.D.,
North Carolina Central University,
Clarence E. Davis, Ph.D.,
North Carolina Central University,
and Dorothy M. Singleton, Ph.D.,
North Carolina Central University

INTRODUCTION

One of the most effective ways for combatting injustices of segregation in the 1960's was the strategy of sit-ins staged by African American youth across the country. The history of sit-ins began with the actions by four African American freshmen from North Carolina Agricultural and Technical College on February 1, 1960 at a Woolworth store in Greensboro, NC. It is important to note that these four men didn't expect to be served at the lunch counter, but as Lewis (2004) writes of the statement by one of the students, "We believe, since we buy books and papers in the other part of the store, we should get served in this part." These four young men—Jibreel Khazan (formerly Ezell Blair Jr.), Joseph McNeil, Franklin McLain, and David Richmond—were determined to change the Jim Crow laws. Complacency was no longer a choice among African Americans. Change had to take place in a nonviolent way. Sit-ins spread across the nation; Woolworth's five-and-dime stores were the targets for the majority of the sit-ins in the southern-most part of the United States. The commitment of these four African American youth, along with thousands of other students in the Greensboro and other surrounding counties, ultimately led to the desegregation of the F. W. Woolworth lunch counter (in Greensboro, NC) on July 25, 1960 (Separate is not equal, n.d.). Unfortunately, there were other Woolworth lunch counters in the south that still remained segregated after the passage of the Civil Rights Acts of 1964.

SIT-INS AS A SILENT PROTEST

A lunch counter at a Woolworth store in the historic city of St. Augustine, Florida was still segregated. St. Augustine is known not only for being the oldest city in America but also as a pivotal site in the civil rights movement. In the 1960's there were six incidents of sit-ins in St. Augustine (March 1960-July 1963) with four of the five occurring at a Woolworth store. The sixth incident involved four individuals, Audrey Nell Edwards, Joe Ann Anderson-Ulmer, Willie Carl Singleton, and Samuel White who staged a sit-in in July 1963. These four young people became known as the St. Augustine Four because of their actions through this ordeal. The young civil rights activists in Greensboro, NC and St.

Augustine were influenced by the non-violent practices of individuals such as Gandhi, early Freedom Riders, and Dr. Martin Luther King, Jr.

During the 1960's, Civil Rights organizers felt that other Civil Rights leaders, from across the nation, should be involved in the movement for social justice. To be reflective of what was happening in St. Augustine, FL and how lives were affected by Jim Crowism and hatred, oppressed people didn't know what to do or what to expect from day to day. Life became uncertain in a confused environment. Due to the attention St. Augustine was getting from the media, several civil rights leaders came to the city to offer support to the protesters.

Mr. Andrew Young was working on behalf of the Southern Christian Leadership Council (SCLC) to help ease the unrest in Saint Augustine, Florida. He was interested in the cause of African Americans having the same rights of White people. He believed in nonviolent protests and upon several instances put himself in harm's way. Young thought violent acts might take place upon the protesters. He really wanted to stop the protest marches because this movement was in the midst of the passing of the Civil Rights Act that had gone through various phases of amendments.

Members from the Southern Christian Leadership Council (SCLC) and the youth organization, Student Nonviolent Coordinating Society (SNCC), were busy all over the country keeping the issue of unfair treatments in St. Augustine known. The youth sit-ins in Greensboro, NC and St. Augustine, FL received some lip service support from national politicians and with the help of media the sights and sounds of the tortures became memorable scenes in the minds of southern and northern people alike. In fact, with the Supreme Court ruling about the Civil Rights Law not being implemented swiftly, many people wondered about the implementation and enforcement of the law.

Watters (1993) writes that unfortunately with the help of media the sit-ins made national news but not the type of news the African Americans desired. He stated, "News coverage continued to ignore the most extraordinary thing about them—non-violence—and continued to emphasize violence" (p.75). The glorification of the violence on the protesters was spotlighted, while the purpose of the protests and the nonviolent stances were mere second thoughts.

POLITICIAN SUPPORT FOR PROTESTERS

In 1960, President Eisenhower expressed sympathy for those who were fighting for the civil rights of African American people. Likewise in 1963, Vice President Lyndon B. Johnson showed support for civil rights when he responded to a request by the President of the local National Association for the Advancement of Colored People (NAACP), Mrs. Fannie Fullerwood, to deny funding for the 400th year celebration in St. Augustine because the event would be segregated. The Vice President stated that wherever he would speak would be integrated. Although his words came true, the venue reverted back to being segregated when the he left town. In spite of the support from politicians, other activists, and SNCC, the sit-in plan used by students in Greensboro and St. Augustine plan was the same.

Cozzens (1998) writes,

> The basic plan of the sit-ins was that a group of students would go to a lunch counter and ask to be served. If they were, they'd move on to the next lunch counter. If they were not, they would not move until they had been. If they were arrested, a new group would take their place. The students should always remain nonviolent and respectful… do show yourself friendly on the counter at all times. Do sit straight and always face the counter. Don't strike back, or curse back if attacked. Don't laugh out. Don't hold conversations. Don't block entrances.

AUDREY EDWARDS TELLS THE STORY

In 2012 at Castillo De San Marcos, Audrey Edwards shared the incidents of that July day in an interruptive program filmed at the Castillo De San Marcos in St. Augustine, FL. (Heinrich, 2012). She explained how she was changed from the inside out over the period of three days in July 1963. She shared how as a high school student she went to school one day and learned that Dr. Martin Luther King Jr. would be preaching at the First Baptist Church that evening and how her family went to hear him. On the way home from church they witnessed people holding signs with the words "Stop Segregation" and "Love and Peace" while at the same time hundreds of Ku Klux Klansmen dressed in robes were beating the people with bats, chains and sticks. She witnessed how dogs had been released on the demonstrators and how the dogs attacked the people.

Edwards may have wondered what the protest was all about. She witnessed demonstrators who were associated with Dr. Robert Hayling, a black dentist in St. Augustine, Florida, who initially had no thought of bringing the Civil Rights Movement to St. Augustine in 1960. He was a recent graduate of Meherry Medical College in Nashville and owed the State of Florida five years of service in exchange for the $1,000 a year supplement he received as a dental student (Prior, 2006). His choices of places to work were Panama City or St. Augustine. He chose St. Augustine. He is hailed as the "father" of the St. Augustine's civil rights movement and ended up fighting to right the injustices of African Americans alongside Dr. Martin Luther King Jr. in the Civil Rights Movement. Hayling is credited as being the person responsible for bringing Dr. Martin Luther King to St. Augustine. During his fight for justice Hayling suffered many horrendous acts of violence at the hands of the Klan. On one occasion they shot through the front door of his home with bullets from a high-powered rifle. They missed his wife and children but killed his dog. No suspects were ever arrested. On another occasion the Klan kidnapped him and one by one broke the fingers on his right hand. According to Prior (2006), Watters (1993) and Duncan (2004) he said, "They knew I was a right-handed dentist, so they beat me up in good fashion." He also stated that 50% of his clients were white and that he recognized some of them in the crowd. Hayling is still unable to extend his middle finger. He was beaten unmercifully and left semi-conscious.

He stated,

> If not for the compassion of a white minister, Reverend Irvin Cheney, who slipped from the rally and called the State Highway Patrol … he and his fellow activists, who were stacked like firewood, would have been burned

alive with gasoline. Dr. Hayling received the most serious injuries, suffering hospitalization for fourteen days, losing eleven teeth, and several broken ribs (Duncan, 2004).

Witnessing the beating and mistreatment of others can be traumatic to anyone, especially a teenager. After witnessing the beatings Audrey Edwards didn't sleep well that night. Psychologists would tell us that this type of traumatic event could affect one's personality. Barber (Dec. 2012) writes in his blog for the Psychology Today journal that "one of the curious features of personality change is that we are more profoundly altered by highly unpleasant experiences than by highly pleasurable ones, possibly because painful experiences signal imminent threats to survival." Audrey knew that the fight for freedom was a fight for survival.

Audrey Edwards continues to share her experiences and relates what happened on the next day at school. Her friends asked if she had heard what happened to Julia. Julia was her fourteen-year-old friend who had taken part as a demonstrator on the day before and had been arrested and taken to jail. Audrey Edwards was distraught. After school her parents allowed her to go with Julia's family to the jail to get her out. Upon arriving at the jail they were told that the demonstrators were not inside the jail but on the side of the building. She was appalled at what she saw. The demonstrators were put in wire chicken coops. Audrey noticed the small jars in the corner of the cage and she knew they had only been given baby food to eat. They found Julia in a corner, afraid and crying. They took Julia home. Once again, Audrey Edwards didn't sleep well.

On her third day of going back to school Audrey Edwards realized that she was different. She looked the same and was happy to be going to school but something was not the same. She perhaps felt an inward change that in some small way is analogous to the rising of Christ on the third day after his resurrection. She had experienced an epiphany. She said her inside change was so strong that the dogs couldn't bite it out of her. The Ku Klux Klan could use water hoses on her and treat her like the dirt in the street and it could not stop her. What was now inside of her could not be beaten out of her. After arriving at school she talked to some of her friends and they all agreed to take part in the sit-in at Woolworth's that day. On the 23rd day of July in 1963, sixteen students, seven of which were teenagers decided to take part in the demonstrations that day. Audrey Nell Edwards (age 16), Samuel White (age 14), Joe Ann Anderson- Ulmer (age 15), and Willie Carl Singleton (age 16) were the juveniles in the group.

Audrey Edwards and her friends were making an adult decision that day. Didn't she know firsthand what had happened to the demonstrators and especially to her friend Julia? The decision to take part in the demonstrations had not been discussed with their parents. This leap into adulthood and knowing the consequences of their actions proved to be a notable act of bravery. However, they had a made up their minds. Nolan (2004) writes that young people during this time formed the shock troops of the Civil Rights Movement, and many efforts were made to suppress them.

As Audrey Edwards continues to tell her story she shares how after school they walked and talked and prayed about what they were about to do. When they arrived at the Woolworth's they followed the rules as most of the other protesters had done in previous sit-ins. They sat quietly and after a few minutes they could hear people shuffling around them. The storeowner shouted insults at them. Audrey remembers a police officer hitting her in the side with a baton. She could still feel the spit on her face from a white woman who said, "We don't serve your kind." She vividly remembered being pulled off of the stool, dragged out of the store and pushed to the ground. The hot breath on her face from a dog and his barking in her ear was so loud that she thought her eardrum would burst. This image is something that would haunt her for years. She and her other juvenile friends were later taken to jail and kept there one month. During the month in jail, their families attempted to bring them food but the guards would not allow them to give it to them. Robert Singleton, Willie's brother, later remarked that they found a way to get the food to them (Bexley, 2006).

According to Bexley (2006) and Nolan (2007) the County Juvenile Judge, Charles Mathis Jr., tried to force the young teenagers to promise that they would take part in no more demonstrations (until they were 21 years old) and that they could get out of jail if their parents signed an agreement saying they would not be involved in demonstrations. The authorities also attempted to pressure them into stating that the movement organizer, Dr. Robert Hayling, was guilty of contributing to the delinquency of minors. Although tactics such as these had been used by law enforcement to humiliate and discourage further demonstrations, the students chose to remain in jail. While facing these difficult times the students had the continued support of their families.

REFORM SCHOOLS FOR THE ST. AUGUSTINE FOUR

After 70 days in a special wing of St. Johns County jail, the boys were sent to Florida Industrial School for Boys in Marianna and the girls to the Ocala Correctional School for Girls (Bexley, 2006). Judge Mathis told the families that he no longer had jurisdiction in the case, and he could not get them back.

In Marianna, Samuel White was working on an electric crew in his school. Willie Carl Singleton was in the machine shop. White said he changed light bulbs and fixed thermostats (Lewis, 2004). A further investigation involving The Florida School for Boys (now the Arthur G. Dozier School) revealed that White and Singleton were spared the horrible atrocities that happened to many other boys. The white boys and black boys were kept in separate buildings. The "White House" on the grounds was known as the place where boys were beaten with a 30 to 42 inch leather strap that was about a half inch to 3/4 of an inch thick. It was weighted or had a piece of sheet metal in the middle. One beaten survivor later commented that the black kids got it twice as bad. Some of the boys did not live through the beatings. As late as 2012, remains of up to 80 boys have been located. Fortunately, on October 21, 2008 The White House was sealed forever (The White House Boys, 2008).

Unlike the reports of abuse to males in Marianna, there were no mention of mistreatments of females at the Colored Girls School at Lowell where Audrey Edwards and Joe Ann Anderson-Ulmer were sent. In an interview with Audrey Edwards and Joe Ann Anderson-Ulmer in 2004 they commented about the jobs they did during the six months in their reform school in Ocala. It was reported: They stated,

> The girls received two shirts, two blouses, two dresses, shoes and one pair of socks in the school... Edwards worked in the cafeteria, and Ulmer joined her after a stint in the principal's office. Their knees were bloodied from scrubbing floors... 'Everything was on our knees,' Ulmer said. 'You could see your reflection in the floor because we cleaned them. Every time you entered a building, you had to buff out. You may walk in, but you have to buff out.' (Lewis, 2004)

In 2004, Joe Ann Anderson-Ulmer remarked that she thought she would be able to be out with the other girls during her incarceration. Instead, they held her in isolation and consequently, she grew to be claustrophobic and even hates elevators (Guinta, 2004). However, the six months stay away from home during the Thanksgiving and Christmas season was unthinkable as a punishment for being a teenage demonstrator. The teenagers just wanted to get back home to their families.

It took the help of the National Association for the Advancement of Colored People (NAACP), with special assistance from Jackie Robinson, a well-known baseball player of the Major Leagues, and the Reverend Dr. Martin Luther King, Jr. to get them released from prison. They were finally released by the action of Gov. Ferris Bryant and the cabinet on January 14, 1964. After their release from reform school, Jackie and Rachel Robinson decided to let the two females of the Saint Augustine Four live with them in Connecticut. They felt that Audrey and Joe Ann needed a place to live for a while other than Saint Augustine, Florida to recover from their ordeal. While away they attended the 1964 World's Fair in New York (Nolan, 2007).

THE CITY OF ST. AUGUSTINE RECOGNIZES THE ST. AUGUSTINE FOUR

In 2004 the St. Augustine Four finally received a proper tribute for their act of bravery and courage for opposing segregation. At that time Willie Carl Singleton had passed away. In 2007 Samuel White passed away. In Dec. 2010, almost 50 years after the civil rights injustices occurred in St. Augustine, Gov. Charlie Crist and the rest of the state Clemency Board issued an apology to hundreds of black civil rights activists (Kam, 2010). In April 2010, the Habitat for Humanity built Audrey Nell Edwards-Hamilton a new home just doors down from where she raised her family ("Home team pitches in," 2008). In 2004, Joe Ann, who lived in Lincolnville, had been a residential instructor at the Florida School for the Deaf and the Blind in St. Augustine for 30 years. In 2005, Audrey Nell Edwards-Hamilton, Joe Ann Anderson and Carrie Johnson co-founded the Embrace Our Youths in St. Augustine, FL. which is dedicated to honoring children for the things they do that add value to their lives and lives of others.

LEGISLATION FOLLOWING THE PROTESTS FOR FREEDOM

In 1964 the Civil Rights Act was passed in the 88th United States Congress effective on July 2, 1964 (PL 88-352). It is considered the most important civil rights legislation since Reconstruction and forbade discrimination on the basis of sex as well as race in hiring, promoting and firing. It is imperative for students to know and understand this important act. The National Archives website (http://www.archives.gov/education/lessons/civil-rights-act/) which is designed to help teachers in the teaching of documents reports the following about some of the language in the Act.

> According to the West Encyclopedia of American Law, Representative Howard W. Smith (D-VA) added the word 'sex' immediately before the Law was passed. His critics argued that Smith, a conservative Southern opponent of federal civil rights, did so to kill the entire bill. Smith, however, argued that he had amended the bill in keeping with his support of Alice Paul and the National Women's Party with whom he had been working. Martha W. Griffiths (D-MI) led the effort to keep the word 'sex' in the bill. In the final legislation, Section 703 (a) made it unlawful for an employer to "fail or refuse to hire or to discharge any individual, or otherwise to discriminate against any individual with respect to his compensation, terms, conditions or privileges or employment, because of such individual's race, color, religion, sex, or national origin." The final bill also allowed sex to be a consideration when it is a bona fide occupational qualification for the job. Title VII of the act created the Equal Employment Opportunity Commission (EEOC) to implement the law.

In addition to important information related to the civil rights events in the 1960's, it is essential for one to be cognizant of documents on which our nation was founded which help make sense of why the St. Augustine Four and others endured the sufferings during that time. One document is The Preamble of the Constitution of the United States of America that states:

> We the People of the United States, in Order to form a more perfect Union, establish Justice, insure domestic Tranquility, provide for the common defense, promote the general Welfare, and secure the Blessings of Liberty to ourselves and our Posterity, do ordain and establish this Constitution for the United States of America (Preamble to the Constitution of the United States).

Likewise the following passage of the Declaration of Independence holds true for the American people who have brought unity through collaborative efforts but has much room for improvement in today's society. The passage is as follows:

> We hold these truths to be self-evident, that all men are created equal, that they are endowed by their Creator with certain unalienable Rights, that among these are Life, Liberty and the pursuit of Happiness. That to secure these rights, Governments are instituted among Men, deriving their just powers from the consent of the governed, That whenever any Form of Government becomes destructive of these ends, it is the Right of the People to alter or to abolish it, and to institute new Government, laying its foundation on such principles and organizing its powers in such form, as to them shall seem most likely to affect their Safety and Happiness. Prudence, indeed, will dictate that Governments long established should not be changed for light and transient causes; and accordingly all experience hath shown, that mankind are more disposed to suffer, while evils are sufferable, than to right themselves by abolishing the forms

to which they are accustomed. But when a long train of abuses and usurpations, pursuing invariably the same Object evinces a design to reduce them under absolute Despotism, it is their right, it is their duty, to throw off such Government, and to provide new Guards for their future security. Such has been the patient sufferance of these Colonies; and such is now the necessity which constrains them to alter their former Systems of Government. The history of the present King of Great Britain is a history of repeated injuries and usurpations, all having in direct object the establishment of an absolute Tyranny over these States. To prove this, let Facts be submitted to a candid world" (Declaration of Independence).

The two passages provide us with the "why" from our past and makes one think back to the four teenagers from Saint Augustine, Florida who were arrested and then sent to reform school for what they thought was right in the "land of plenty." We can better educate our children today about equal rights for all people based on fairness and honesty. Jibreel Khazan (formerly Ezell Blair Jr.), Joseph McNeil, Franklin McLain, David Richmond, Audrey Nell Edwards-Hamilton, Willie Carl Singleton, Joe Ann Anderson-Ulmer, and Samuel White are just a few young African Americans, from different Woolworth sit-ins, who experienced first-hand racism and hatred from White people: one group from Florida and another from the state of North Carolina during the early 1960's. During this time, many African Americans considered this time in history as a "walking time bomb." The Civil Rights Movement took a critical toil on people's lives across the nation.

Much has been learned from the Civil Rights Movement; much has been learned from the Saint Augustine Four.

These four young teenagers sacrificed their lives to enhance the quality of living for all African American people. They were living on the edge, not knowing what would take place or what would happen to them. From their trials and tribulations, many people have learned to accept uniqueness among cultures; they have learned that there are many similarities among cultures than there are differences; and, regardless of geographical differences, people are people.

Note: *Audrey Nell Edwards-Hamilton is the married name of Audrey Edwards. Joe Ann Anderson-Ulmer is the married name of Joe Ann Anderson.*

FOR FURTHER DISCUSSION

The following are thoughts that could generate further discussion of this chapter:

1. Should teenagers/young adults that stand up for social justice and their freedom to express themselves peacefully be placed under arrest?
2. The Civil Rights Movement was initiated as a peaceful, non-violent movement; should opponents have the right to inappropriately attack peaceful protesters? Why/why not?
3. If a student had to portray one of the four young teenagers, how would that person have presented him/herself during these terrible times of discrimination and Jim Crowism?
4. If a student had to write a reflection of what took place during the civil rights movement of the 1960s and re-

late it to the 21st century, how would that student approach writing an account of this movement? Or would there be a movement?

5. Based on the Constitution of the United States of America, are the words true for all people? Give an example.

REFERENCES

Barber, N. Trauma resets personality. (December 2012). Retrieved from http://www.psychologytoday.com/blog/the-human-beast/201212/trauma-resets-personality.

Bexley, K. (May 15, 2006). 'St. Augustine Four' honor brave mothers. Retrieved from staugugstine.com/stories/051506/news_3834185.shtml.

Civil Rights Acts 1964. An Act. July 19, 1964. University of Southern Mississippi. Retrieved from http://digilib.usm.edu/cdm/ref/collection/manu/id/3689.

Cozzens, L. (25 May 1998)."The Civil Rights Movement 1955-1965." *African American History.* Retrieved from http://fledge.watson.org/~lisa/ blackhistory/civilrights-55-65/sit-ins.

Duncan, G. (2004). Veterans of the civil rights movement—Dr. Robert B. Hayling. Retrieved from www.crmvet.org/info/staug1.htm.

Declaration of Independence. Retrieved from www.ushistory.org/Declaration/document.

Guinta, P. (May 16, 2004). Ceremony to honor students' civil rights action in '63. Retrieved from http://staugustine.com/stories/051604/new_2322764.shtml.

Heinrich, R. (July 22, 2012). The St. Augustine Four. Retrieved from http://www.youtube.com/watch?v=QDW6xRhrq40.

Home Team Pitches In: Civil rights advocate getting habitat home. (2008, April 22). Retrieved from http://staugustine.com/stories/042208/community_txt01_005.shtml.

Kam, D. (2010, December 9). Fla. Clemency board expresses 'profound regret' for 1960s civil rights arrests. *The Palm Beach Post.* Retrieved from http://www.palmbeachpost.com/news/news/state-regional/fla-clemency-board-expresses-profound-regret-for-1/nLnTr/.

Lewis, K. (2004, May 31). For the St. Augustine Four, civil rights war
    began with order for burger. Retrieved from http://jacksonville.com/
    tu-online/stories/053104/met_15742537.shtml.

Nolan, D. (2004). Veterans of the Civil Rights Movement - The St. Au-
    gustine Four. Retrieved on from www.crmvet.org/info/staug2.htm.

Nolan, D. (2007). ACCORD Freedom Trail. Retrieved from
    www.accordfreedomtrail.org /four.html.

Prior, R. (February 19, 2006). Civil rights activist was on the front lines.
    Retrieved from http://staugustine.com/stories/021906/new_3648063
    .shtml.

Separate is Not Equal. (n.d.) Smithsonian National Museum of American
    History, Behring Center. Retrieved from http://americanhisto-
    ry.si.edu/brown/history/6-legacy/freedom-struggle-2.html.

The Preamble to the Constitution of the United States of America. Re-
    trieved from www.ushistory.org/documents/constitution.htm.

The White House Boys (2008, October 21). The sealing of the White
    House Torture Chamber. Retrieved from http://youtu.be/K_
    sgo3gZzyM.

Watters, P. (1993). Down to now: Reflections on the southern civil rights
    movement. Athens, GA: University of Georgia Press.

4

STOKELY CARMICHAEL

The Rise of "Black Power"

By Clarence E. Davis, Ph.D.,
North Carolina Central University,
Nancy Reese-Durham, Ph.D.,
North Carolina Central University,
and April Holbrook, M.Ed.,
North Carolina Central University

INTRODUCTION

The Civil Rights Movement of the 1950's and 1960's looked to change the unjust treatment of people who were regarded as subordinate because of a disposition towards a restrictive American ideology. People were scorned, beaten, and murdered because of prejudicial perceptions about gender, race, national origin, ethnicity, and religious beliefs. Americans were at a crossroads. There were people who used tactics of fear and hate to oppress the uneducated and the minority, while others no longer able to stand this tyranny, stood up and became determined to be heard and seen as equals. During this time of unrest, nonviolent protests and interracial alliances began to take flight and so began what is known as the Civil Rights Movement; however, not all leaders embraced the ideologies of nonviolence and such alliances. Stokely Carmichael would become such a leader advocating the use of any means necessary to regain a stolen freedom.

THE ORIGINS OF A LEADER

Stokely Standiford Churchill Carmichael was born in the home built by his father, a master carpenter, and two of his father's friends in Port of Spain, Trinidad. Born June 29, 1941, Stokely Carmichael was the only male and middle child of Adolphus and Mabel Carmichael. In October 1944, Mabel Carmichael, left her husband and three children and traveled to the United States. Adolphus followed Mabel to the United States, approximately a year and a half later, leaving all three children to be cared for by relatives. At the time of his father's departure, Stokely Carmichael was about 5 years old.

For the next six years, young Carmichael lived with his father's sisters and paternal grandmother. It was through this matriarchal support system in which much of his early years became defined. Six months after the death of his beloved grandmother, in June of 1952, Stokely Carmichael departed for the United States of America.

In September of 1952, Carmichael began his journey through the American education system at P.S. 39 in New York. To his surprise, school was not as he had imagined; however, after a brief cultural adjustment, Carmichael found his footing. One encouraging note for young Carmichael was that he realized he could compete with his peers academically, and in many instances he excelled. Before the end of his fifth grade year, the Carmichael family moved to another neighborhood in the Bronx, causing Stokely to finish that year at P.S. 34. During his 7th and 8th grade years, young Carmichael thrived at P.S. 83, but it was not until he was in the Bronx High School of Science and was becoming a young adult that his future views would begin to take shape.

At the Bronx School of Science, Carmichael experienced a more diverse population of students along with a vaster social and political climate than he had been exposed to, at previous institutions. It was during this time he became aware of the "radically cultural streams" (Carmichael & Thelwell, 2003) that were shaping the man that he was to become. These cultural streams, in addition to the views of the cultural views of Bronx Science, were that of the predominantly white catholic neighborhood in which he lived. In addition, young Carmichael was fashioned by the Caribbean culture and community that was his family's social and ancestral background, the trek he took with his father every 2-3 weeks to a Harlem barbershop, and his love of music which enlightened him to the plight of African Americans during the mid-1950's.

AN ACTIVIST EMERGES

During his junior and senior years at Bronx Science, Carmichael became aware of Dr. Martin Luther King Jr.'s nonviolent protests. While Dr. King's struggle earned little praise in some of Carmichael's circles of activism, Carmichael, himself, at the time, respected Dr. King's efforts as effective.

"I supported any strategy that could move the Southern masses of our people to confront American apartheid. And any leader who could inspire them to this kind of direct action had my complete respect" (Carmichael & Thelwell, 2003, p. 111).

In the spring of 1960, during Carmichael's senior year, the Sharpeville Massacre occurred in South Africa. While reports vary, nearly 250 nonviolent protesters were either killed or wounded by the South African police and military. These protesters were marching against the pass laws which were used for segregation and the monitoring of non-whites. It was hurtful, violent attacks on his people, such as the one in Sharpeville, which caused young Carmichael to take notice of the plights of others. It was during a protest in Washington, D.C. that he became introduced to Howard University and the Nonviolent Action Group (NAG). The NAG was an affiliate of the Student Nonviolent Coordinating Committee (SNCC). Given Carmichael's family wishes for his future and his own personal political fire, it later became cemented in his mind where he would go to college.

Although not a recognized student organization at Howard University, NAG positioned itself to become the voice denouncing the tyranny of African-American oppression. Carmichael recalled that during his studies at Howard, the university benefited from scholars and thinkers who were shunned by other predominantly white institutions of higher education. The predominantly white institutions, in many cases, held racist attitudes refusing to educate or employ black scholars.

"For at Howard, we had the immense benefit of a number of venerable, pioneering, scholarly presences as well as brilliant young scholars and artists who today might undoubtedly be seduced by the wealth and 'prestige' of the Yales and Stanfords of the academic world" (Carmichael & Thelwell, 2003, p. 127).

As a student, Carmichael's experiences expanded both broadly and with depth. From his small semi-sheltered world in the Bronx, he soon experienced life at Howard that pushed his ideals, made him think, and allowed him opportunities to explore life through the eyes and knowledge of others. He was exposed to different political and cultural understandings, and he had to develop his identity and beliefs as they related to these life experiences. As other students and professors began to stimulate and influence young Carmichael, he came to the realization of the struggles that were ensuing African-Americans dealt with preserving and advancing legacies, as well as defining their identities in a country that treated them as lower-class citizens.

The members of NAG, especially Carmichael, saw their work as something that was beyond a mere student movement. It was seen as an organization mostly of students that were engaged in a fight against racism in society. The members gained insight in challenging the status quo through their continued conflicts with administration at Howard University. All be it indirectly, the Howard University administration presented the members of NAG an informal education on the freedom of speech, freedom of assembly, and political action. It was during these unintended lessons where Carmichael and the other members of NAG developed their skills in political maneuvering. These skills would soon be tested outside of the safety of the university.

FREEDOM RIDERS

In 1961, a change was on the horizon. This change would bring nonviolent protests into the living rooms of Americans and test the fabric of civilized society. The effects of this change, known as the Congress of Racial Equality (CORE) Freedom Rides, would change the lives of the protestors and define NAG and SNCC and its role within the Civil Rights Movement. The idea behind the CORE Freedom Rides was to challenge the Supreme Court's ruling requiring the integration of facilities for interstate travelers. These rulings, even though they were long established laws, they were ignored. To face this challenge, blacks and whites would travel together from Washington D.C. to New Orleans, Louisiana on public transportation. When Carmichael first heard of the plan he was not sure the rides would prevail. There were so many ways the CORE plan could fail. There were so many ways the plan could be marginalized and the attempt would fade away. On May 4, 1961, while he was not one of the original thirteen riders, Carmichael bid Godspeed to several friends who were on the two departing buses.

Stokely Carmichael's concern, as well as many of the others, was that this nonviolent protest would surely face violent opposition. It became evident this fear would have to be confronted by the original thirteen if the movement was to go forward. So determined were some of the original thirteen to face this opposition, a few even made out their last will and testaments. The first reports about the riders appeared optimistic, even when trouble materialized in South Carolina it still seemed hopeful that while continuing on their way to Georgia the obstacles that they were going to face were not going to be as bad as some originally thought. However, in Georgia the group was warned that members of the Ku Klux Klan were organizing to confront the Freedom Riders in Alabama. Armed mobs met the two buses in Anniston, Alabama and again Birmingham, Alabama. The Freedom riders were beaten and brutalized. Some riders were brutalized so horrifically that they were left to die in pools of their own blood and they never recovered completely. In Birmingham, it became evident the buses they were traveling in were no longer a viable option for the riders. They decided to finish the trek by flying to New Orleans. Because of the chaos that ensued when the riders went to the airport, it took nearly 20 hours, and only after a liaison from the Department of Justice intervened, for the riders to catch a flight to New Orleans. The CORE Freedom Ride had ended.

Carmichael, himself, would soon be on a flight to New Orleans, and with others, the plan was to take up the purpose and intent of the original riders. He was to land in New Orleans and meet up with a group that would be going into Mississippi by train, testing the railroad system. As Carmichael and the group approached the train station they received shouted insults, were spat upon, and had objects thrown at them. Through this turbulence the group prevailed and reached the train. As they got on the train, rocks and other debris were thrown through the windows of the train. When the train arrived in Jackson, Mississippi, Carmichael and the group were arrested as they were waiting in the "whites only" waiting room. It was here that nineteen year old Carmichael was first arrested. As more Freedom Riders were arrested, they were all housed within the same unit of jail. At night, the Riders would sing defiantly. These songs were moving and cemented the unification of the political prisoners. Prison administrators fearful of an uprising from the regular prison population, shipped the Freedom Riders off to one of the most brutal penitentiaries within the south, Parchman Farm Penitentiary. By the end of June, over 160 Freedom Riders had been convicted in Jackson, Mississippi, with many of them sent to Parchman Farm.

While residing in Parchman, Carmichael maintained his stance of nonviolent protests. He and others were continuously subjected to inhumane treatment; however, the members of the group found strength within themselves and each other. In discussing some of treatment the riders received, David Fankhauser, a Freedom Rider that was sent to Parchman Farm Penitentiary, was quoted as saying:

> "In our cells, we were given a bible, an aluminum cup and a tooth brush. The cell measured 6 × 8 feet with a toilet and sink on the back wall and a bunk bed. We were permitted one shower per week, and no mail was allowed. The policy in the maximum security block was to keep lights on 24 hours a day" (Fankhauser, 2002).

In July of 1961, shortly after his twentieth birthday and forty-nine days after his arrest, Carmichael was bonded out of Parchman by CORE. The protestors were released with the stipulation the group leave the state immediately. Instead of leaving the state, Carmichael and others were received by group of individuals who welcomed the Freedom Riders with a lavish reception celebrating their heroic sacrifices.

A VISION OF EMPOWERMENT

Because of his experiences at Parchman Farm Penitentiary, Carmichael was invited by CORE to speak at several fund-raising and awareness functions while recuperating in New York. It was during this time when young Carmichael began his transition from being a political activist to becoming a leader in political activism. Nearly one month after his release from Parchman, Carmichael was invited to participate in a political seminar at Fisk University. This seminar would alter the course for many SNCC and CORE members.

The CORE Freedom Riders, although publicly supported, were somewhat of an embarrassment to the Kennedy Administration. Looking for a way to curb the intransigent views of some SNCC and CORE members, the Kennedy Administration began talk with top leaders in the Civil Rights Movement. The purpose of these meetings was to find ways to shift efforts from direct confrontational tactics to something that the current administration could support and protect: voter registration. This was seen by many members of SNCC and CORE, including Stokely Carmichael, as an obvious political ploy. During the 1960 Presidential Election, John F. Kennedy won the popular vote by less than one-half of one percent. Many attributed Kennedy's success to a large, last minute, surge of black votes. Therefore, some saw this stratagem as a way for the Kennedy Administration to build a stronger, broader base of support in the Southern states, particularly with black voters.

Voter registration was supposed to serve several purposes, as mentioned earlier, one of which was to increase the black voter support of the current administration in the south. It would empower black southerners who had been betrayed during the political wrangling of the Compromise of 1877. And, with the administration behind them, activists, like Carmichael, would be offered more support and protection for their participation of organizing the southern black voters. By taking advantage of this opportunity, Carmichael and others could confront the methodical disenfranchising of people who had suffered almost a century of malfeasance, discrimination, brutalization and murder, and degradation.

One of the first tests in which SNCC would face for black voter registration and mobilization would be in the town of Albany, Georgia, in September of 1961. Albany, Georgia was a segregationist stronghold (D'Angelo, 2001). Many of the streets in black neighborhoods were unpaved and the homes of many blacks were denied access to the city's sewage lines. Even though blacks represented about 40 percent of the population of Albany, Georgia, only 20 percent of the black community had registered to vote. The Albany Movement is noted as being one of the first mass movements within the Civil Rights Era (Formwalt, 2003), with mass demonstrations that included common citizens as the protesters. On November 17th of 1962 the Albany Movement officially began with a coalition of community groups including the NAACP Youth Council and the Negro Voters League. Within days three student protesters were arrested for refusing to leave a bus station dining room, two others were arrested for entering a whites-only waiting room. On November 25th the first mass meeting was held and for weeks following this meeting several protests continued throughout Albany to challenge the segregationist regime. In December, when a group of students were arrested for defiantly and openly entering the wrong side of a railroad terminal, over 400 students marched in protests of the arrests. Although not involved in the initial desegregation effort, Martin Luther King Jr., and the Southern Christina Leadership Conference (SCLC) members, in mid-December, lent their support for the Albany movement. A rift soon emerged as members of SNCC were offended by King's involvement because they felt as if King's and the SCLC's methods were too placid. While King worked with the Albany Movement, the media focused on his nonviolent protest principles and his "no bail" strategy of completely filling the local jails with protesters. Ultimately, King would describe the Albany movement as a failure; However, Cobb (2008) points out that the success in Albany was that the people were empowered and voter registration and mobilization efforts would lead to a run-off election in which one of the contenders was a black businessman. In addition, segregation statutes were removed from the city commission books and Albany led the way for disenfranchised people within the surrounding counties to seek empowerment.

FREEDOM SUMMER

Although Carmichael was still in school when the Albany Movement officially began in November of 1961, he began to wrestle with his desire to help more with the movement and go to school. During his second year back at Howard, he would lend support to the movement as time and his studies permitted. Sadly, in January of 1962, Carmichael's father, Adolphus Carmichael died unexpectedly. Carmichael's mother became the sole provider for the family and through hard work and determination she continued to help pay for Stokely's education. It was no longer an issue *if* Carmichael would stay in school and graduate, but *when* and *how* could he help with the movement knowing the sacrifices his mother was making for his education.

The summer after his father's death, Carmichael returned to Mississippi. It had been almost 11 months since his release from his 49 day captivity at Parchman Farm Penitentiary. In June of 1962, in Leflore County, Greenwood, Mississippi, Carmichael worked at the Greenwood SNCC office aiding in the voter registration and mobilization movement. It quickly became obvious to Carmichael that the Mississippi Delta Blacks were living in substandard conditions. The healthcare and educational system in the Mississippi Delta were virtually nonexistent. It was in Mississippi, from the early to mid-1960s, that Carmichael would call his base of operations. During the summers, Carmichael and others would register black voters and teach basic mathematics and literacy skills to black children in Mississippi. This effort would become part of a much larger movement known as Freedom Summer.

The project, Freedom Summer, was a student run project that originally took its lead from SNCC. It later became a united effort including SNCC, NAACP, CORE, and SCLC. These groups worked together under the umbrella of the

Council of Federated Organizations (COFO). After the assassination of Medgar Evers in June of 1963, hundreds of students were organized to register black voters, for a real election—the 1964 presidential election. The goal of Freedom Summer was to organize black voters and address the deplorable education of many black children. The organization of the black voters would allow black representation in areas where, even though they were largely populated by blacks, few, if any held offices in local, district, and state government. The strategy was that during summers, SNCC would use student volunteers from colleges and universities throughout the nation to increase voter registration and to help rural blacks gain a better education through literacy and mathematics programs. Although racial tensions and injustices faced these young men and women, they remained diligent to the causes of voter registration and desegregation. Carmichael, himself, was arrested numerous times while working for SNCC. One of the most infamous acts against Freedom Summer workers was when three civil rights workers, two white and one black disappeared. It was later discovered that the three were murdered and their bodies buried on a farm. The potential for horrific acts, such as this, faced young volunteers, like Carmichael, on a regular basis.

In 1964, Stokely Carmichael graduated from Howard University with a Bachelor of Arts degree in Philosophy. Upon graduating from Howard, there was little thought about what Carmichael wanted to do, and when he was offered a job with SNCC, it seemed providential. Carmichael would continue with Freedom Summer in Mississippi. After helping in the registration of almost 60,000 black voters, the COFO helped to create a new political party called the Mississippi Freedom Democratic Party (MFDP). In 1964, at the Democratic National Convention (DNC) Credentials Committee, Fannie Lou Hamer from MFDP would openly and passionately denounce the all-white delegation from Mississippi and request fair representation at the DNC. The MFDP was extended only two nonvoting at-large seats, which was less than their initial request. Some, Martin Luther King Jr. of SCLC and Roy Wilkins of the NAACP, felt as if this was a symbolic victory for the MFDP (D'Angel0, 2001). The MFDP rejected the offer and returned to Mississippi. Down, but not out, Fannie Lou Hamer and the MFDP would return and be seated at the 1968 DNC. Again, tensions between SNCC and SCLC surfaced during political maneuverings at the 1964 DNC Credentials Committee, as the SNCC supported MFDP's stronger stance and rejection of the offer from the committee. The success of the Freedom Summer project was that it achieved an unprecedented number of voter registrations and thousands of youths, who were at the Freedom Schools, received a better education than they had previously been able to receive.

MARCHING ON

In July of 1964, President Johnson signed the Civil Rights Act, which in essence stated that black citizen's civil rights needed federal protection and it was illegal to discriminate against someone based on a person's race or gender. This cleared the path for the Voting Rights Act, in August of 1965, also signed by President Johnson, which abolished several obstacles that had previously discouraged many blacks from voting. These two important pieces of legislation aided SNCC in their fight against the white-southern oppression of black citizens. While SNCC and other organizations had the law on their side, the enforcement of the law, within the south, still remained a central concern for many volunteers. In May of 1966, Stokely Carmichael would replace John Lewis to become the chairman of the SNCC. Carmichael had earned this position through his hard work during several marches and movements, and his continued dedication to the Freedom Summer Project and Freedom Schools. Carmichael was seen, by many, as a logical replacement as he had first-hand accounts and knowledge of the struggles occurring in the south. He had faced dozens of arrests in fighting for the rights of the disenfranchised and he had personally experienced the brutality of this undertaking. Given SNCC's evolving dissatisfaction with the SCLC's and Martin Luther King's nonviolence and integration principles, Carmichael's forthrightness and experiences would help move SNCC to a more unrestrained docket.

In June of 1966, James Meredith, the young man who helped to integrate the University of Mississippi, led marchers on the "March against Fear" demonstration from Memphis, Tennessee to Jackson, Mississippi to help raise voter registration awareness. On the second day of the March, Meredith was shot twice by gunman with a shotgun. Carmichael (SNCC), King (SCLC), and Floyd McKissick (CORE) within days took up Meredith's march, calling it "Meredith's March against Fear." The group soon became thousands. Thousands of people joined the demonstration and made the over 200 mile trek toward Jackson. On June 25, James Meredith joined the demonstrators for the final day of the march.

By the time Carmichael and the nearly 15,000 demonstrators reached Jackson, Mississippi they had registered over 4,000 voters. However, it was on the stop in Greenwood, Mississippi, ten days before the official end of the march in which Carmichael would ascend to a place of legend in the Civil Rights Movement and become the civil rights leader he was destined to become.

It happened on June 16, 1966 when the "Meredith March against Fear" demonstrators tried to set up camp in Greenwood, Mississippi and Stokely Carmichael was arrested for the 27th time. He was arrested and held in jail for trespassing on public property. When released several hours later, an enraged Carmichael gave his first "Black Power" speech. The SNCC had been looking to develop a new slogan, and with Willie Ricks urging Carmichael to "Drop it now. The people are ready. Drop it now," (Carmichael & Thelwell, 2003, p. 507) that was when Carmichael took his stand. Cleveland Sellers, Jr., a SNCC volunteer, Civil Rights Activist, and Carmichael friend recalled:

> When Stokley moved forward to speak, the crowd greeted him with a huge roar. He acknowledged his reception with a raised arm and a clenched fist. Realizing that he was in element, with his people, Stokely let it all hang out.
> 'This is the twenty-seventh time I have been arrested—and I ain't going to jail no more!'
> The crowd exploded into cheers and clapping.
> 'The only way that we gonna stop them white men from whuppin' us is to take over. We been saying freedom for six years and we ain't got nothin'. What we gonna start saying now is Black Power!'

The crowd was right with him. They picked up his thoughts immediately.

'BLACK POWER!' they roared in unison." (Carmichael & Thelwell, 2003, p. 507).

While immediately controversial and having connotations that are seen as both negative and positive, the term mentioned and coined by Carmichael, "Black Power" was a call for a people to take a stand and to be recognized. This was a call for black people to take charge of their own destinies and govern themselves. Many people, including Martin Luther King Jr., saw Carmichael's words as an open aggression and opposite to the principle of nonviolence protests. Martin Luther King Jr., while at first calling Carmichael's call for action a poor choice of words, did eventually acknowledge that because of the things Carmichael had experienced and been witness too, it appeared reasonable for Carmichael to want to set aside the nonviolent principles that King believed (The Martin Luther King, Jr. Research and Education Institute , n.d.).

THE STORY CONTINUES...

Controversy began to follow Carmichael afterwards, and later in life, through various controversies he remained true to his beliefs. Although Stokely Carmichael was the chairman of SNCC, he lost the position about one year later. In 1967, he made controversial trips to Communist Cuba and China, as well as Vietnam. From 1967-1969, Carmichael was the prime minister of the Oakland-based Black Panther Party (The Martin Luther King, Jr. Research and Education Institute, n.d.). For the next thirty years, Carmichael would remain the type of leader and activist who was not afraid to make sacrifices because it was the right thing to do. In the late 1970's, Carmichael would change is name to Kwame Ture. In November of 1998, close to forty years after stepping up to become a member of the second wave of Freedom Riders, Stokely Carmichael lost his fight to cancer. And while the slogan "Black Power" is probably better remembered as a call for empowerment during the civil rights movement, it is because of our unsung hero, Stokely Carmichael that this phrase has any meaning today.

POINTS OF DISCUSSION

The following topics could be considered for extensive research and discussion:

1. Research and discuss how the Oakland-based Black Panther's Party got its start from the SNCC involvement in Lowndes County, Alabama.
2. Research and discuss the different controversies that followed Stokely Carmichael after his famous "Black Power" speech.
3. Research and discuss the relationship Stokely Carmichael had with other presidents of SNCC: Marion Berry, John Lewis, and Charles McDew.
4. Research and discuss the original Freedom Riders and how they continued to contribute to the Civil Rights Movement.

5. Research and discuss the different ideologies of SNCC, the SCLC and other organizations, such as the NAACP.
6. Create a timeline and map for important events during the Civil Rights Movement.

REFERENCES

Carmichael, S., & Thelwell, E. M. (2003). *Ready for revolution: the life and struggles of Stokely Carmichael (Kwame Ture)*. First Scribner.

Cobb, Charles, E. Jr., (2008). *On the road to freedom: A guided tour of the civil rights trail*. Algonoquin Books.

D'Angelo, R. (2001). *The American civil rights movement: Readings and interpretations*. McGraw-Hill/Dushkin.

Fankhauser, David B. (2002, February 7). Freedom rides: Recollections by David Fankhauser [webpage]. Retrieved April 2, 2013 from http://biology.clc.uc.edu/fankhauser/Society/freedom_rides/Freedom_Ride_DBF.htm#skin%20on%20steel.

Formwalt, Lee W. (2003) Albany Movement. *The New Georgia Encyclopedia*. Organization of American Historians. Retrieved April 2, 2013 from http://www.georgiaencyclopedia.org/nge/Article.jsp?id=h-1057.

Span, P. (1998). The undying revolutionary. *The Washington Post*. Washington, DC. Retrieved March 27, 2013 from http://www.washingtonpost.com/wp-srv/politics/campaigns/junkie/links/carmichael.htm.

The Martin Luther King, Jr. Research and Education Institute (n.d.) Stokely Carmichael. Retrieved March 27, 2013 from http://mlk-kpp01.stanford.edu/index.php/encyclopedia/encyclopedia/enc_stokely_carmichael_1941_1998.

5

JACKIE AND RACHEL ROBINSON

Continuing the Legacy

By Brenda Martin, Ph.D.,
University of Arkansas at Pine Bluff,
and Clarence E. Davis, Ph.D.,
North Carolina Central University

INTRODUCTION

Many people only remember Jackie Robinson as a champion athlete who faced personal struggles as being the first African-American to sign a major league baseball contract. However, the story and contributions of Jackie and Rachel Robinson go beyond just baseball and into philanthropic activities, entrepreneurship and rising to become an advocate during the Civil Rights Movement. Although Jackie's baseball legacy predates the integration of the United States Army and the Brown v. Board of Education decision (William & Sielski, 2004) his Civil Rights Movement began in the 1940s and his contributions to society should never be forgotten.

JACKIE: THE EARLY YEARS

Jack Roosevelt "Jackie" Robinson, the youngest of five children, was born January 31, 1919 in a sharecropper's cabin in Cairo, Georgia. His parents, Jerry and Mallie Robinson, were sharecroppers and worked on the Susser plantation. When Jackie was less than 2 years old, Jerry Robinson became frustrated with farming in the south and left his wife and five children. Mallie and the children (Edgar, Frank, Mack, Willie Mae, and Jackie) were forced to leave their cabin at Susser's, since their living there relied on Jerry's working in the fields on the plantation. Mallie and her children moved in with her brother, Burton, at his home in Pasadena, California. To support her family, Mallie found work cooking and cleaning in the homes of white families (Robinson, 2004). Even though she was able to eventually save enough money to move from her brother's home, Mallie and the children remained one of the poorest families in their new predominantly white neighborhood. Discrimination and segregation would follow the Robinsons to California. While California was not as openly or harshly segregated, as it was in the deep-south, many Californians were still racially intolerant and several white neighbors were angry about the Robinson's moving into the neighborhood. Growing up, young Jackie experienced discrimination. He had rocks thrown at him and was insulted routinely. His wife described Jackie's experiences growing up:

> "Jackie grew up in Pasadena, California, where discrimination was even more blatant and humiliating. For instance, he could not swim in the YMCA pool, except on a

day for Negroes. So, Jack experienced discrimination in a much more powerful form" (Scholastic, 1998).

Jackie attended Muir Technical High School in Pasadena. Jackie developed into a great student-athlete and participated in several sports including football, basketball, track, baseball and tennis during his high school years. He lettered in four of these sports while in high school. After high school, while wanting to remain close to home, Jackie enrolled at Pasadena Junior College in 1937.

In 1939, Jackie transferred to the University of California at Los Angeles (UCLA). He was active in four sports, becoming the first in the history of UCLA to make the varsity team in four sports: football, baseball, basketball, and track and field (Robinson, 1996). While at UCLA, Jackie would become smitten with a nursing student named Rachel Isum. It was love at first sight and he proposed almost immediately after meeting her.

RACHEL: THE EARLY YEARS

Rachel Annetta Isum was born in Los Angeles, California on July 19, 1922 to Charles Raymond and Zelle Isum. Rachel mentioned that, while growing up as a child although she was subjected to segregation, it was not as harsh as the treatment received by others.

"Racial discrimination was very subtle. For instance, if we went to the movies, as we entered the lobby, the usher would direct us upstairs to the balcony. We were being segregated almost without knowing it" (Scholatic, 1998).

After graduating high school, Rachel entered into the nursing program at UCLA. She would earn her Bachelor's degree in Nursing, while Jackie served in the Army. She would later marry Jackie Robinson in 1946. She continued her education, earning a Master's degree in psychiatric nursing from New York University. Rachel Robinson would work for several years advancing within the healthcare field and eventually she would teach for the nursing program at Yale University.

LIFE AFTER UCLA

Sadly, in 1941, Jackie Robinson would lose his athletic scholarship at UCLA and leave the university before he earned his degree. He would play semiprofessional football, first with the Honolulu Bears and then with the Los Angeles Bulldogs. Although when drafted for military service in 1942, he was absolved due to an ankle injury, Jackie's patriotism pressed him to enlist in the Army.

Jackie excelled in the Army, quickly becoming a corporal. However, Jackie soon became frustrated by the lack of opportunities for African-Americans to become officers. After pressure from an investigation, Jackie was admitted into officer's school in Camp Hood, Texas, where he would later become a second lieutenant. It was in Texas that Jackie would fall victim to discrimination from the Jim Crow Laws. On a trip to the hospital for his ankle, Jackie was ordered to sit at the back of the bus. He refused and was later court martialed for numerous charges, including failure to obey a direct command and disrespect toward a superior officer.

Although charged with nearly a dozen offenses, he was found not guilty of each wrongdoing. However, even though decency prevailed, Jackie no longer wanted to be in the army and he was later honorably discharged in 1944.

After leaving the Army Jackie would play professional baseball for the Kansas City Monarchs, a Negro League team. In April of 1945, unknown to many, Jackie would audition to play for the Boston Red Sox. Although he was not allowed the opportunity to play for the Red Sox, Branch Rickey, the general manager of the Brooklyn Dodgers, signed him to play for the Montreal Royals, a minor league team. Rickey chose Jackie, not because he was the best player, but because Jackie possessed qualities that could be helpful in the integration of Major League Baseball. It was Rickey's plan to integrate baseball and he needed someone who could cross the color barrier and be acceptable to both Whites and African-Americans. The qualities that made Jackie the best candidate were that he grew up in a predominantly white neighborhood, competed in athletics with white students, and he was contrary to the racist views of the "uneducated black" (Foster & LifeCaps, 2012). In 1947 Jackie Robinson would become the first African-American to play Major League Baseball. Later that year, Jackie would be named Rookie of the Year, and within two years, he would be the National League's Most Valuable Player.

Jackie Robinson's integration of the Major Baseball Leagues was not easy. He experienced discrimination not only from other teams and fans, but also from his teammates. He could not stay in the same hotel with his team when traveling to various cities for scheduled games. Jackie experienced many insults and was taunted. People tried to hurt

him because he was the only African-American on a Major
League Baseball team. And even though by 1949 Jackie was
an established roster player, the Ku Klux Klan tried to pre-
vent him from playing games in Atlanta, Georgia (Foster &
LifeCaps, 2012). Because of these incidents, Jackie some-
times found it hard to honor his pact with Branch Rickey, in
which he would not respond to provocation. It would not be
until the early 1950's that Rickey would allow Jackie Robinson to conduct himself as the other white players could
which empowered him to behave as he pleased. During an
interview on February 11, 1998, Mrs. Robinson stated that
the lesson they learned was, "if you have an overriding goal, a
big goal that you're trying to achieve, there are times when
you must transcend the obstacles that are being put in your
way. Rise above them. Jack wanted to integrate athletics"
(Scholastic, 1998).

In facing this goal, Jackie would learn to become more
than just a ball player, he became or would become a symbol
of hope. The Robinsons would become beacons for change
and leaders in a much larger movement against racial injustice and inequality.

CIVIL RIGHTS MOVEMENT

In 1953, Jackie accused the New York Yankees franchise of
racial prejudice, in that the Yankees had no African-
American players on their team. This accusation harmed the
perception of one of the most lucrative franchises in the
American League and Jackie was summarily asked to report
to Commissioner Ford Fick's office. Fick ordered Jackie to

remain composed while in public and to be more selective with his words. This incident goes to prove that while the leagues were officially integrated in 1947 that even after six years, there were still differences in how the players were treated due to the color of their skin. Even after his retirement in 1956, Jackie remained a supporter in the integration of all sports.

Immediately after retiring from baseball, Jackie accepted the position of Vice President of Personnel for Chock Full O'Nuts. Chock Full O'Nuts is a coffee shop franchise mainly throughout New York and eastern states. This position allowed him to enhance the personnel program to better assist African-American employees. He became very knowledgeable on benefits, wage scales, and training. He talked to the employees to solicit information and identify problems. His commitment to making life better for below management level employees resulted in extensive training, promotions to managerial level, and better pay for employees who worked the shop's counters (Robinson, 1996).

Jackie used his celebrity status to aid in voter registration. Roy Wilkins, executive director of the National Association for the Advancement of Colored People (NAACP), asked him to serve as chairman of the Freedom Fund Drive. Jackie traveled across the country to raise money and awareness for voter's rights. He was paired with famed lawyer Franklin Williams, and the two men created an energy felt by all who heard them speak. The Southern Christian Leadership Conference (SCLC) held a dinner in Jackie's honor at the Waldorf-Astoria Hotel. Jackie insisted that all the proceeds of the dinner go to the SCLC's voter registration drive in the South (Robinson, 1996). The SCLC's voter registration drive was to empower African-Americans in the deep-south to register and mobilize during election times. To get people to vote was to get people to take a stand for their own future.

In his continued support of the Civil Rights Movement, in 1957, Jackie sent a letter addressed to President Eisenhower commending him on his decision to send troops to Arkansas to protect the first nine African-American students to be enrolled at Little Rock Central High School. Although the decision was long overdue, Jackie's letter expressed the impatience felt by many African-Americans during this publicized crisis. After meeting with presidential candidates Richard Nixon and John F. Kennedy in 1960, Robinson publicly endorsed Nixon because he believed Nixon's civil rights record was more promising than Kennedy's record (National Archives and Records Administration, 1997; Robinson, 1996). In a 1961 letter to President Kennedy, Robinson expressed his belief that the President was moving in the right direction with regards to civil rights, but hinted that African-Americans had waited too long and that a faster pace was needed to make progress. Robinson felt it was his duty to use his status as a Baseball Hall of Fame inductee to inform politicians on the struggles and injustices of African-Americans plaguing the country (National Archives and Records Administration, 1997).

The Robinsons watched as the civil rights of African-Americans were being abused at every turn, especially in the South. In 1963, they held a jazz concert at their home to raise bail money for demonstrators who were jailed during the Birmingham, Alabama demonstrations. Nationally known artists Duke Ellington, Dave Brubeck, Dizzy Gillespie, and the Adderleys performed at the concert. A total of

$15,000 was sent to Martin Luther King, Jr. and the SCLC to provide support for the activists. The annual concert provided support for the Civil Rights Movement for many years (Robinson, 1996; Scholastic, 1998). In addition, the Robinsons did not shelter their children from the discussion of fairness and injustice. The entire family participated in the March on Washington on August 28, 1963.

In January of 1964, Jackie Robinson, Reverend Dr. Martin Luther King Jr., and the NAACP pressured the governor of Florida to release four youths, Joe Ann Anderson, Audrey Nell Edwards, Willie Carl Singleton, and Samuel White, who were arrested in 1963 during a nonviolent, sit-in demonstration at a local Woolworth's lunch counter. The four youths, who were local high school students, would later be known as the "Saint Augustine Four." Upon the release of the St. Augustine Four from reform school, Jackie and Rachel Robinson opened their home to the two female students. The Robinsons relocated the two girls to their home in Connecticut, with the hope that Audrey and Joe Ann could regain some resemblance of a normal life after the horrific ordeal these two students faced. It was their intention to help the girls recover at a place, other than Saint Augustine, Florida (Nolan, 2007).

By continuously looking for ways to help improve the lives of African-Americans, Jackie began to focus his efforts on economic development and political power. Along with other activists and investors, he charted the Freedom National Bank in 1964. At the time, it was the only African-American owned and operated commercial bank in the state of New York (Robinson, 1996). Jackie Robinson continued to keep the members of the White House focused on the Civil

Rights Movement. Six months before his death, Robinson wrote a letter to Richard Nixon's Presidential Assistant, Roland Elliott, urging him to inform the President to listen to African-American youth and to be more aggressive in ending injustice (National Archives and Records Administration, 1997).

On the morning of October 24, 1972, Jackie Robinson died of a heart attack. He was 53 years old. It seems fitting that Robinson (1996) in reflecting on his life shared the belief of Frederick Douglass, "If there is no struggle there is no progress" (p. 223), and "I am one of the fortunate ones granted a mission at the age of twenty-three, a great partner, and the spirit to prevail" (p. 223).

THE STRUGGLE CONTINUES

In 1972, the Jackie Robinson Construction Company began to house families with low and moderate incomes. The company built a 197-unit apartment in Yonkers, N.Y. After Jackie's death, Rachel Robinson resigned from Yale University and became president of the construction company. She reorganized the company as the Jackie Robinson Development Corporation, which would focus on real estate development. A joint venture was formed with Halpern Building Corporation to build Whitney Young Manor in Yonkers, as Jackie had contracted earlier. The company would later collaborate with Halpern and the New York State Urban Development Corporation to build and manage 1,300 units of low-and moderate-income housing in Yonkers, Brooklyn, and Manhattan (Robinson, 1996).

In a 2007 interview with USA Today about corporate diversity, Rachel Robinson provided insight on race as it relates to the corporate environment. When asked if Jackie would be pleased about diversity in the workplace, Mrs. Robinson replied that her husband was an advocate for change. Even though Jackie had witnessed progress, he would want to see more progress towards equality. Mrs. Robinson also mentioned that some corporations participate in diversity efforts for recognition, while other corporations apply sincere recruiting and training strategies for minorities. A critical section of the interview, contributing to the resilience of those who fought for civil rights, was when Mrs. Robinson was asked if Jackie ever said he would have performed better if fans had been tolerant. Rachel simply said that he had to cope with all types of negative behaviors.

"No one could attack his high self-esteem. The hostile environment challenged him to do better. Jackie Robinson had to excel to show them that they were wrong. He had to meet the challenge for our race" (Scholastic, 1998).

The Jackie Robinson Foundation (JRF) was established in 1973 to provide education and leadership development opportunities for minority youth. This living legacy of Jackie Robinson encompasses the persistent leadership and the focus on providing opportunities for minorities that mirrors the life of its namesake. The foundation provides valuable resources related to navigating through higher education, leadership, public service, and financial assistance.

Jackie and Rachel Robinson's commitment to be catalysts for social change and civil rights advocates can be summed up with this statement from Mrs. Robinson's 1998 interview with Scholastic, "…if someone is homeless, uneducated, without medical care, without support, I have to feel some responsibility for them, and do whatever I can think to do" (1998).

Jackie Robinson was a man of integrity and Rachel Robinson was a woman of strength. They were both kind, patient, and tried hard to be positive role models for all Americans. Jackie Robinson's baseball jersey number "42" was retired June 4, 1972 from Dodger Stadium; and April 15 of every year it has been proclaimed as Jackie Robinson's Day. Jackie and Rachel Robinson were visionaries. They focused on embracing the well-being of all people, especially the underserved people in this nation (Simon, 2002).

POINTS OF DISCUSSION

The following topics could be considered for extensive research and discussion:

1. Other than baseball, what other sports faced color-barriers and who were the pioneers in those sports?
2. Research and discuss the relationship that Jackie Robinson had with other leaders during the Civil Rights Era?
3. Research and discuss the career path of Rachel Robinson.
4. Compare and contrast Jackie Robinson's contributions in sports to Arthur Ashe, Tiger Woods, and Charles Follis.
5. Research and discuss the "gentleman's agreement" that existed in major league baseball from 1897 to 1947.

REFERENCES

Foster, Frank and LifeCaps (2012). 42: A Biography of Jack "Jackie" Robinson. BookCaps.

National Archives and Records Administration (1997). Beyond the Playing Field: Jackie Robinson, Civil Rights Advocate. Retrieved from http://eric.ed.gov.

Nolan, D. (2007). ACCORD Freedom Trail. Retrieved from www.accordfreedomtrail.org /four.html.

Robinson, R. (1996). Jackie Robinson: An Intimate Portrait. New York, N.Y.: ABRAMS.

Scholastic (1998). Interview with Rachel Robinson. Retrieved from http://www.scholastic.com/teachers/article/interview-rachel-robinson.

Simon, S. (2002). In Chapter: Jackie Robinson and the integration of baseball. John Wiley &

Son, Inc: Hoboken, NJ.

The Jackie Robinson Foundation (2002). Rachel Robinson: Oral History Archive [Video Recording]. Retrieved from http://www.visionaryproject.org.

Williams, P. & Seilski, M. (2004). How to be like Jackie Robinson: Life lessons from baseball's greatest hero. Health Communications, Inc.; Deerfield, FL.

SUMMARY

The unsung heroes played an integral part in the Civil Rights Movement in the 1960s and thereafter. Has the dream been deferred? No. There are many unsung heroes today who are very active in the trenches. Do we still believe in the cause to make things better in America? Yes. Is there racism in America today? Sure it is. There is subtle racism which is running rampant throughout the United States of America and the world.

America is a land of plenty; being able to embrace people from different nationalities; cultures; and different religions. The most notable form of racism has been toward African Americans since slavery. Over 150 years, racism has been gnawing at the flesh of people of color. Many attempts have taken place to eradicate it from our society. The Civil Rights Movements quickly moved throughout the nation with such leaders as John Lewis, Malcolm X, Huey Newton, Reverend Dr. Martin Luther King, Jr., Reverend Jesse Jackson, Rosa Parks, Reverend Ralph Abernathy and many others, to name a few.

Some the Civil Rights Act of 1964 was passed with the then President of the United States of America, Lyndon B. Johnson. This act brought some relief to people of color, especially to the African American communities across the nation. However, times were still hard for individuals looking for employment. African Americans continued to be treated like second class citizens. They were still experiencing poverty, discrimination, and institutional racism. At this time, they felt there was no hope in sight for them to move forward in a positive way. People who were hiring did not look like them. So the odds were against them.

Although substantial gains had been made with the passing of the Civil Rights Act, African Americans felt that much more promising situations must occur for them. Many turned to furthering their education; for they wanted a good life; they wanted a piece of the American pie (prosperity; fulfillment of dreams; education, etc).

Where are African Americans today and their outlook on accomplishing the American Dream? They are achieving much success; more African Americans are seeking college degrees; race relations are improving; and an African American U.S. President is now in office, Barack Obama. Let's keep hope alive.

ABOUT THE EDITOR

Dr. Dorothy M. Singleton is a full professor in the School of Education at North Carolina Central University. She has written several articles, book chapters, and book reviews related to several education topics. Dr. Singleton, along with other colleagues, has written a book on *The Aftermath of Hurricane Katrina: Educating traumatized children Pre-K through college.* She is also Editor of a journal. Dr. Singleton has presented at a number of national and international conferences.

Dr. Singleton attended Shaw University in Raleigh, NC where she earned her bachelor's degree in Elementary Education; and earned a master's degree in Elementary Education with a concentration area in History at North Carolina Central University in Durham, NC. She continued to complete her doctorate (Ph.D.) in Curriculum & Instruction with an emphasis in Special Education/Language Impairment at the University of South Florida-Tampa.

She is a product of the Civil Rights Movement during the 1960s. She participated in several non-violent activities while in high school in Tampa, Florida, and while in undergraduate school in Raleigh, North Carolina. The whole idea of Jim Crow laws frightened her as she traveled from Tampa, FL to Raleigh, NC by Greyhound Bus. Her mother taught her all the *rules of what to do* and *what not to do* if she had to encounter White people during her traveling. She will never, to this day, understand why American people were so divided along racial lines.